REMARKABLE CHILDREN

Louis Braille

THE BLIND BOY WHO WANTED TO READ

A Picture-Book Biography

The information for the Remarkable Children Series was gathered from old letters, journals, and other historical documents.

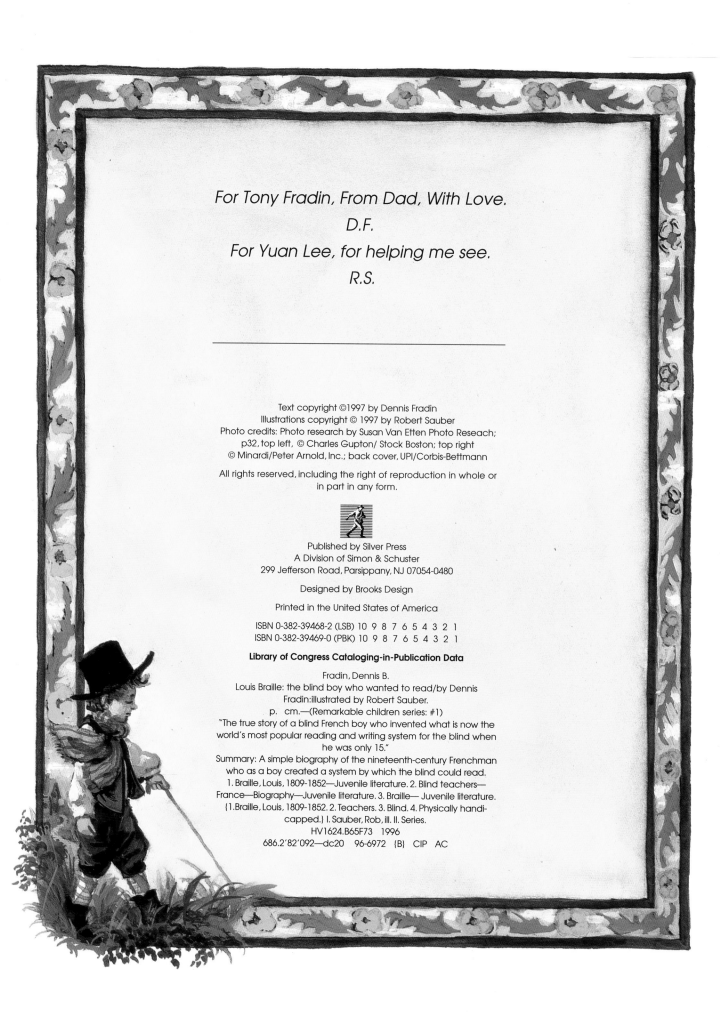

For Tony Fradin, From Dad, With Love.
D.F.
For Yuan Lee, for helping me see.
R.S.

Text copyright ©1997 by Dennis Fradin
Illustrations copyright © 1997 by Robert Sauber
Photo credits: Photo research by Susan Van Etten Photo Reseach;
p32, top left, © Charles Gupton/ Stock Boston; top right
© Minardi/Peter Arnold, Inc.; back cover, UPI/Corbis-Bettmann

Published by Silver Press
A Division of Simon & Schuster
299 Jefferson Road, Parsippany, NJ 07054-0480

Designed by Brooks Design

Printed in the United States of America

ISBN 0-382-39468-2 (LSB) 10 9 8 7 6 5 4 3 2 1
ISBN 0-382-39469-0 (PBK) 10 9 8 7 6 5 4 3 2 1

Library of Congress Cataloging-in-Publication Data

Fradin, Dennis B.
Louis Braille: the blind boy who wanted to read/by Dennis
Fradin:illustrated by Robert Sauber.
p. cm.—(Remarkable children series: #1)
"The true story of a blind French boy who invented what is now the
world's most popular reading and writing system for the blind when
he was only 15."
Summary: A simple biography of the nineteenth-century Frenchman
who as a boy created a system by which the blind could read.
1. Braille, Louis, 1809-1852—Juvenile literature. 2. Blind teachers—
France—Biography—Juvenile literature. 3. Braille— Juvenile literature.
{1.Braille, Louis, 1809-1852. 2. Teachers. 3. Blind. 4. Physically handi-
capped.} I. Sauber, Rob, ill. II. Series.
HV1624.B65F73 1996
686.2'82'092—dc20 96-6972 {B} CIP AC

REMARKABLE CHILDREN

Louis Braille

THE BLIND BOY WHO WANTED TO READ

*The true story of a blind French boy who invented
what is now the world's most popular reading and
writing system for the blind when he was only 15.*

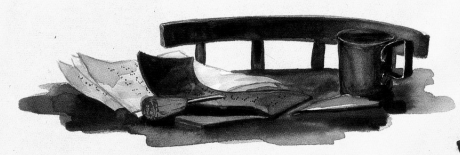

BY DENNIS FRADIN • ILLUSTRATED BY ROBERT SAUBER

Silver Press

Parsippany, New Jersey

The year 1809 began happily for the Braille family of Coupvray, France. On January 4, a boy was born to Monique and Simon Braille in their moss-covered stone farmhouse. The couple named him Louis, pronounced LOO-ee in French. The Brailles were a loving family, and the child with the bright blue eyes and curly blond hair was fussed over by the entire household.

Besides his parents, Louis had a brother who was fourteen years older than he and two sisters who were sixteen and eleven years older. Louis could usually find someone to play games with him and tell him bedtime stories. And there was always someone for Louis to help as the family did their daily tasks.

As soon as he could walk, Louis followed his brother out to the barn and helped him feed the chickens and milk the cow. He accompanied his mother and sisters out to the purple fields and helped them tend the grapes. But Louis's favorite pastime was to work alongside his father.

Simon Braille was the village's saddle and harness maker. Louis spent many hours in the workshop next

to the farmhouse, watching his father cut, shape, and stitch the leather. Simon let Louis play with his extra leather scraps. He even let his youngest child pound on the leather scraps with a mallet. But he warned Louis that he must never, ever touch his sharp tools!

One day when Simon wasn't looking, Louis's curiosity got the best of him. The three-year-old picked up an awl—a tool used to punch holes. Louis tried to poke the awl through his leather scrap as he had seen his father do, but he wasn't strong enough. Finally, Louis stabbed at the leather scrap with all his might. Before he knew what had happened, the awl glanced off the leather and pierced his left eye.

Simon Braille reached the screaming boy first, followed quickly by the rest of the family. Simon and Monique stopped the bleeding with a cloth. Then Louis's parents bandaged and patched his injured eye.

Had this accident happened today, Louis would not have lost all of his vision. Doctors might have even saved his damaged eye. But in 1812, people did not yet know about germs. An infection lodged in Louis's injured eye and spread to his good eye. The

blue of the sky, the purple grapes in the fields, his family's faces—everything gradually faded out to Louis. By the age of five, Louis Braille was totally blind.

In Louis's time, most blind people had miserable lives. Since they couldn't communicate with others by reading or writing, it was considered useless to send them to school. As a result, they were cut off from such professions as teaching, law, and medicine. Many blind people had to live in poorhouses. Others begged for food and money on street corners. The lucky ones found jobs shoveling coal or carrying bricks in exchange for food and a place to sleep. Simon and Monique Braille vowed that Louis would never become a beggar or a human beast of burden. For their blind son, life would continue as normally as possible.

Simon Braille cut down a tree branch and carved it into a cane for Louis. At first a family member had to help the boy feel his way around the house. Soon, however, he learned a few tricks to help him navigate on his own. Louis counted the number of steps from room to room. He whistled or sang so that he could locate walls, by the echo. Once Louis could tap his

way around the farm without help, his parents assigned him several household tasks, such as setting the table at mealtime and filling the bucket with drinking water at the well.

His family also began to take Louis on walks through the countryside and into the village. "What do you think of the weather?" his father or mother would ask, as they passed through the fields. "It looks like rain" or "The sky is clear today," he would reply, depending on how the sun and air felt on his skin. In town he learned where the bakery was by its smell of bread and where the blacksmith's and carpenter's shops were by the sounds within. Louis amazed many of Coupvray's six hundred people by greeting them by name before they said a word. He knew them by the sounds of their footsteps and by remembering where they lived or worked.

Despite his blindness, Louis even learned to read and write a little. His oldest sister, Catherine, made the letters of the alphabet out of straw and taught him to identify them by touch. Once Louis knew his letters, Catherine showed him how to make words.

Louis and his family sat in the kitchen and exchanged straw messages many an evening.

Soon after Louis's sixth birthday, a new priest came to the village of Coupvray. Upon meeting the Brailles, Father Jacques Palluy was so impressed with Louis that he became his private tutor. Louis began tapping his way to church where he studied with the young priest in the garden. Father Palluy taught him to identify birds by their songs and flowers by their smell. The boy also had a talent for memorizing the poems and Bible stories that Father Palluy read to him. But Louis yearned for more than knowledge. He wanted to attend school like other children his age.

Father Palluy helped Monique and Simon persuade the teacher at the village school to accept Louis as a student. Each day a classmate stopped by the Braille house to walk with Louis to the one-room schoolhouse. Louis was a brilliant student. He was often the first to solve a difficult math problem, and he remembered the teacher's lessons word for word. The only subject he could not succeed at was reading. While his classmates read aloud from their books,

Louis could only sit and listen. To Louis Braille, reading books seemed like the greatest thing in the world—and the least possible for a blind person.

By 1819 Louis was ten years old and had attended the village school for three years. In those days very few blind children—and not many with vision—went to school longer than that. Father Palluy and the schoolmaster thought that Louis should continue his education at the National Institute for the Young Blind in Paris. Founded in 1784 as the world's first school for blind children, the institute would further Louis's education and teach him skills so that he might earn a living. To Louis, however, the most exciting news was that the institute had special books the blind students could read.

Simon and Monique had many a talk about Louis. They didn't want to send him to live with strangers in a big city, yet they knew that the institute was a great opportunity for him. In the end, they decided to do what was best for Louis, which meant letting him go.

On a February morning in 1819, Louis walked with his family to the stagecoach stop in Coupvray.

The tears and kisses flowed when the coach arrived. Louis and his father then climbed aboard and began the 25-mile trip to the French capital.

Louis's excitement and nervousness grew as the horses pulled the carriage along. After a four-hour journey, he and his father were dropped off at the outskirts of the city. Never had Louis heard such a bewildering mixture of voices and noises as he experienced on the walk to the institute. Finally he and his father arrived at the big building at 68 Rue Saint Victor. Simon spoke briefly to school officials before saying good-bye to his ten-year old son. When Simon left the school to return to Coupvray, he also closed the door on Louis's childhood. For, aside from occasional visits home, Louis would live at the institute for the rest of his life.

For the first few days, Louis was sorry that he had come to the school. He placed his clothing, with a box of pastries his mother had sent along as a treat, under his dormitory bunk. On the very first night when he felt under the bed, he found that his pastries had been stolen. A boy in a nearby cot named Gabriel Gauthier

explained that, as a new student, Louis could expect more such tricks. He was right. Louis's classmates thought it was funny to lock him in the bathroom and to lead him into a closet when he thought he was entering a schoolroom.

Gradually, though, Louis grew to like the institute. Gabriel became his friend and helped him count the steps from his bunk to the classrooms and from the bathroom to the dining hall. Louis excelled in his subjects, and showed a gift for playing the piano and organ. In the school's workshops he learned to make purses and baskets. He also enjoyed the outings to the Paris parks where the boys explored the flower gardens and listened to the quacking ducks. But what Louis looked forward to most was his turn to read the special books in the school library.

Valentin Hauy, founder of the institute, had arranged to have several books printed using raised letters. After a few months, Louis was allowed to read the books. But the thrill of reading quickly faded. For one thing, it wasn't easy to tell an *m* from an *n* and an *i* from a *j*, which made the method as slow as his

BOARD OF EDUCATION DIST. 25
ARLINGTON HEIGHTS, ILL.

family's way of sending messages with straw letters. Also, since each letter had to be big enough to be felt by touch, the books were bulky. A typical book had to be divided into twenty volumes, each weighing 20 pounds, so that the whole thing weighed 400 pounds.

By the age of eleven, Louis had read all fourteen of the institute's raised-print books. He wanted to read more books, but none were available. Louis realized that there would never be very many books for the blind without a simpler way to represent letters.

Louis began experimenting with various codes. In the evenings, he sat on his bunk and used a knitting needle to punch holes in paper. When he returned home on vacations, he went to his father's workshop like he had done as a little boy. While Simon made saddles, Louis used the awl or another sharp tool to poke holes in leather scraps. Louis made shapes, mathematical signs, and other symbols to represent letters. However, his codes were no easier to figure out by touch than Hauy's raised letters.

Officials at the institute did not take Louis's efforts seriously, for how could a blind boy invent a

better reading method than the school's founder? Louis was starting to think they were right when, one day in 1821, Captain Charles Barbier came to speak at the institute. Barbier had invented night writing, a method of representing sounds with raised dots and dashes on paper. By feeling the dots and dashes, soldiers could read messages without having to light a lantern on the battlefield. Captain Barbier hoped that night writing could also help blind people.

Although it was too complex for creating books, night writing gave twelve-year-old Louis an idea. Dots and dashes were small, easy to feel, and quickly made on paper with a tool called a stylus. Louis began to experiment with ways of writing words with dots and dashes. The boys in the dormitory learned to fall asleep to the sound of Louis making dots and dashes with his stylus. Night after night, month after month, Louis continued his work. He finally completed his system after three years' work and showed it to his fellow students in the fall of 1824. They loved Louis Braille's method, which they named Braille for him.

Louis Braille was only fifteen years old when he invented his system that would bring the world of books and knowledge to millions of blind people.

Louis soon decided to get rid of the dashes and use from one to six dots to represent each letter. By feeling the number and the position of the dots, the reader determined which letter was intended. Louis taught his classmates to read and write Braille, which they used to pass notes and to write stories. But Louis had much grander plans in mind for Braille.

In 1826, at seventeen, Louis graduated from the institute and became a teacher there. He made extra money by playing the organ at a nearby church. Much of his salary went to pay people to copy books into Braille. He himself worked thousands of hours copying the works of Shakespeare and other authors into Braille. Someone with vision read to Louis while he made the dots. Over the years, Louis built a library of Braille books, which he lent to the institute's students.

New Braille books couldn't be made fast enough as far as the blind students were concerned. However, school officials were jealous that the invention of a

fifteen-year-old boy was replacing their raised-print books. For years the Braille system was outlawed at the school. A student later explained: "We had to learn Louis Braille's alphabet in secret, and when we were caught using it, we were punished."

In 1843 the principal burned a number of books printed in Braille and gathered up the students' styluses. Louis was heartbroken, yet refused to give up. He and his students wrote new books in Braille, sometimes using nails and forks to make the dots. The principal saw that the students would never give up Braille. He approved its use for the institute in 1844, the same year that the school first admitted girls. It had taken Louis twenty years to have his Braille system accepted by his own school.

Louis spent the rest of his life trying to introduce Braille to the world. He demonstrated Braille to wealthy people in Paris who applauded, but did little to help the method catch on. He also wrote to scholars and officials, but his efforts were generally ignored.

By his thirties, Louis was ill with tuberculosis. Many stories are told of his kindness and generosity

in his last years. He donated much of his salary to blind children so that they could attend the institute. And even as he lay sick in bed, he continued to write Braille books for the institute's young people.

On January 6, 1852—two days after his forty-third birthday—Louis Braille died. At the time, he was better known as a church organist than as the inventor of a reading system for the blind. But as the years passed, Braille was adopted by nation after nation. In 1917 the United States became one of the last developed nations to approve Braille for general use.

Today Braille is the most popular reading and writing method for the blind. Millions of people all over the world read books, magazines, and newspapers produced by Braille printing presses. Children with vision problems read Braille textbooks. Blind people send Braille greeting cards, wear Braille wristwatches, use Braille computers, and take elevators that have Braille directions.

Today blind people take part in the mainstream of life thanks to Louis Braille, the blind French boy who wanted to read.

HOW THE BRAILLE ALPHABET IS USED

The Braille alphabet has helped to open the world to the blind. Besides books, Braille is used for magazines and greeting cards, on elevator and computer controls, and even Braille watches. As Louis Braille said "Blind people must be treated as equals, and communication is the way to bring this about."

a	b	c	d	e	f	g	h	i	j	k	l	m
n	o	p	q	r	s	t	u	v	w	x	y	z